WHAT PEOPLE ARE SAYING ABOUT

A Prayer Primer for Catechists and Teachers

"Gwen Costello's new book, *A Prayer Primer for Catechists and Teachers* is both the fruit of a woman of faith's prayerful reflections and a wonderful resource for contemporary educators. It is full of powerful prayer experiences guaranteed to enrich your prayer life. Simple, profound, touching, down-to-earth, inspiring are a few words that can be used to describe this wonderful book. It gives a perfect 'hands on' approach that so many religion teachers today are seeking as well as words of wisdom to deal with such perennial issues as how to respond to children who complain that 'Mass is boring.' The section on ritual is a 'must' read for catechists and religion teachers."

Bridget Mary Meehan
Author, *God Delights in You* and *Prayers, Activities, Celebrations (and More) for Catholic Families*

"This engaging book presents practical, well-tested ways of experiencing prayer oneself as well as ways of teaching prayer to children. Gwen Costello sets out to introduce children to a personal god, beyond knowing facts about God. This she accomplishes well, by suggesting steps to prepare oneself to communicate with God and entering into conversation with God."

Joan Metzner, M.M.
Poet and author of *Plucking the Strings: A Personal Psalm Journal*

"A refreshing book of quiet, gentle beauty to help you s-t-r-e-t-c-h and grow—no matter where (or who) you are."

Ginger Farry
Author, *A Teacher's Prayerbook*

"This book indeed gives 'simple and basic information about personal and class prayer'; but it goes well beyond the expected! Very detailed directions for a variety of prayer experiences are given, encouraging even a new catechist or religion teacher to experiment with different and fresh new approaches to prayer."

Margrit A. Banta
Pastoral Minister at Holy Trinity Church, Norfolk, VA
Author, *Parish Reconciliation Services*

"When I read this book, I had the feeling that the author was speaking directly to me, inviting me personally to deepen my awareness of God's presence and to proclaim it joyfully to the world. Catechists will be energized and inspired by Ms. Costello's personal, warm style and will appreciate her practical, yet creative, suggestions for inviting children into a relationship with God. Obviously an experienced pray-er and catechist herself, Ms. Costello offers specific and detailed directions for using various forms of prayer in the classroom. Anyone who prays or leads children in prayer will want this book!"

Carole MacClennan
Author, *Learning By Doing*

"Gwen Costello's *Prayer Primer for Catechists and Teachers* is a resource that will guide catechists and teachers on their own faith journey as they lead students to seek a spiritual direction in today's world. Practical suggestions and positive activities make this book a must for every religious educator's book shelf."

Phyllis Wezeman
President, Active Learning Associates, Inc.
Author, *20 Prayer Lessons for Children,*
20 More Prayer Lessons for Children, and
Guiding Children through Life's Losses

GWEN COSTELLO

A Prayer Primer

for Catechists and Teachers

for Personal and Classroom Use

TWENTY-THIRD PUBLICATIONS
BAYARD ⊕ Mystic, CT 06355

Dedication

I dedicate this book
to all the teachers, catechists, aides,
office helpers, volunteer parents,
DREs, and principals
I have worked with
over the years…

in loving and grateful
recognition of all
the great work you do.

Third Printing 2002

Twenty-Third Publications
A Division of Bayard
185 Willow Street
P.O. Box 180
Mystic, CT 06355
(860) 536-2611
(800) 321-0411

ISBN 0-89622-922-X
Library of Congress Catalog Card Number 97-62565
Printed in the U.S.A.

Contents

Introduction

I have encountered many catechists and religion teachers over the years, and I am always inspired by their willingness to take on the role of "proclaimer" of the gospel. I feel humbled by such generosity of spirit and I am encouraged by their example. And though I often get requests to speak to groups of DREs and catechists, I always feel that I can learn more from them than they can learn from me.

Nevertheless, I still get asked. The nature of my work as a full-time editor (with ever-present deadlines) keeps me from saying yes. And so I decided to "speak" in the way I know best—through this *Prayer Primer.* It says what I would say in person, could I be where religion teachers are.

I am not a theologian and my point is certainly not to present a theology of prayer. Rather, I am a practitioner, someone who has been laboring in the "field" for more than thirty years. I have taught in parochial schools, volunteered as a catechist, and I have worked as a DRE for many years, first in a diocese and then in various parishes. I know from experience how important prayer is in the life of a "proclaimer," and that's precisely why I want to share the message in this book.

I call it a "Primer" deliberately because it offers simple and basic information about personal and class prayer. There are many excellent books that cover these topics in great depth, and I encourage you to pursue them when you have the time and interest. In the meantime, if these words motivate you to pray more often and to share prayer more enthusiastically with those you teach, this little book will have done exactly what it was meant to do.

Chapter One

Your Own Prayer

Your role as a teacher of the faith is to keep the "vision" of faith alive and to connect those you teach with other Catholics in the living of it. In other words, we not only offer our children someone to believe in; we also offer them the support and example of a believing community. Our role in this is not as complicated as it might seem because it is based on two essential beliefs: Jesus *came among* us at the incarnation, and at the Last Supper, he promised to *stay* with us.

> I will not leave you orphans... The Advocate, the Holy Spirit that the Father will send in my name will teach you everything and remind you of all that I have told you (John 14:18–26).

The Holy Spirit, the Spirit of the Risen Christ, is among us—right here, right now, in this place and time. This is "the" vision of the church. And so, our first and foremost responsibility as catechists is to proclaim the presence of the risen Christ who is always with us through the Holy Spirit.

We do this officially in the classroom or other teaching spaces, but our role as proclaimers doesn't stop there. We are called as Christians to live this vision daily, in our homes with our families, in our workplaces with our coworkers, in our neighborhoods with our friends and neighbors, in our parish community with other believers—wherever we are. The key question then is how do we say to people through our daily words and actions (and especially those we teach) that we believe in the presence of Christ?

Prayer Is Saying Yes

A good place to start is with our own personal prayer. Prayer is saying yes to God's presence, saying welcome and thanks to what already is. Just as fish live in water, so we live in God. God is always with us. Prayer does not make God present; rather, it is our personal response to the sacred and holy that is already within us.

Jesus taught this through parables and through his own life choices. An obvious example is the prodigal son: the implication of this well-loved parable is that God is watching for us, waiting for us with arms open wide. The gospel of Luke says:

> And the father, seeing the son while he was still a long way off, was deeply moved. He ran out to meet him, threw his arms around him, and kissed him (Luke 15:20).

And recall the words that Jesus spoke at the Last Supper:

> "When that day comes, you will know that I am in my Father, and that you are in me, just as I am in you…I will ask the Father, and he will give you another helper, the Spirit of truth, to stay with you forever" (John 14:20).

These words are complemented by those in the letter to the Romans:

> The Spirit comes to help us, weak as we are.

For we do not know how we should pray; the Spirit pleads for us in groans that words cannot express. And God who sees into our hearts, knows what the thought of the Spirit is (Romans 8:26–28).

We Can Communicate with God

While our initial reaction might be that there is no way for us to adequately communicate with God, in these passages Jesus tells us otherwise. Not only does God dwell within us and speak to us, we have been given the Holy Spirit as our personal translator. The Spirit knows what we need, and then pleads for us in groans that words cannot express. God who sees into our hearts, knows the thought of the Spirit.

Prayer moments are times to get in touch with this vision of our faith. The Mass, our public parish prayer, is one very important way to pray; celebrating the sacraments is another. But there are also more simple daily ways to be in touch with the Holy Spirit "in whom we live and move and have our being." One of these is the prayer of quiet or meditation.

A Four-Step Process

I would like to describe for you a simple four-step

method that you can use as a preparation for meditation or even contemplation (which at its simplest is "feeling AWE in the presence of God"). This form of prayer is particularly important for religion teachers who are always communicating with others about the things of God.

Step One Choose a quiet prayer place. This can be any place, a special room or a special chair in a room. The important thing is that you are away from interruptions. Get comfortable and then consciously breathe God's presence in, and breathe out anything that is upsetting, troubling, or distracting. Do this over and over until you feel calm and relaxed. (Breathing by the way, is one of the best ways to call ourselves back into God's presence. Think about it, when you take a deep breath you have to focus on it. It brings you back to the present moment.)

Step Two Recall your favorite prayer or prayer words, and recite these silently over and over, for example: Come Holy Spirit; Lord Jesus Christ, Son of the Living God, have mercy on me; or Glory to God. Alleluia.

Step Three Put aside any books or papers and imagine yourself going into a peaceful place where God is waiting for you. (Note: Picture God in whatever image is most comfortable for you: God, Jesus, Holy Spirit, creator, friend, savior, etc.) As you move into this place, repeat your prayer word or phrase.

Step Four Rest with God. Imagine that you have arrived in that peaceful place and God has greeted you as a beloved friend might. Savor this realization and open your heart to whatever God might speak to you. The purpose of this moment is not to be thinking about God, but to be absorbed in God, to rest in God.

An Experience that Calms

When you have tried this several times, I hope that this will be an experience that calms and quiets you. I hope that it will put you in an attitude of readiness to respond to God who loves and welcomes you always.

You can practice a combination of these steps in the following way. Place your hands on your knees, open palms up. Imagine that your open palms are a prayer. This gesture itself can be your prayer. It says, "O God, you know all my needs, spoken and unspoken. Fill me with your presence." With palms thus open, rest with God in your heart and mind.

This is a simple and easy prayer method for teachers. When you feel frustrated, get off task, or become overly critical of a child in your class, just pause and place yourself back in God's presence by placing your hands on your knees for a moment or two. God knows what this means and knows what you need.

Praying with Scripture

Another way to grow in awareness of God is through Scripture. Never mind that you are teachers and catechists, people who lead others in faith matters. It can still be a daunting task to use the Bible in prayer. There is so much about the past, and so much about the people who wrote the biblical words that we don't know. There are customs, rituals, nuances, and even words and phrases that are unfamiliar to us.

And yet this is the Word of God, the one we are challenged to share with children and teenagers. How do we begin to make sense of it?

We can only take one step at a time, and I would like to suggest a simple process here that might help you to gain insights and information about any given Scripture text. Ordinarily, you won't do all four steps in one sitting. I recommend that you use them as part of the process of lesson planning, especially when your lesson centers on a Scripture passage or story.

Step One Choose a Scripture text. This, as just

mentioned, could be one that you will use in your next lesson. Take time to read this text at least twice, slowly and reflectively, and then put it aside.

Step Two (This would ordinarily take place a day or so later.) Look at the Scripture passage again. This time make note of its place in the Bible and look it up. Read the paragraphs before and after it. If there are any footnotes about the text in your Bible, read them. Also note the setting. Where does this story or passage take place? Who are the people involved? What are the circumstances?

Place Yourself There

Step Three This time approach the passage through "prayer of imagination." Place yourself in the setting. Picture the people in it. Imagine what the circumstances might have been and try to "feel" them. Close your eyes and spend three minutes silently reflecting on what is happening to you. How does what you are seeing and feeling influence your faith?

Step Four Spend time praying over the Scripture passage. You have read it, reflected upon it, and placed yourself within it. Now you are ready to listen to what God is saying to you through it. Don't force this step, just remain quiet, open, and prayerful so that God might speak to your mind and heart.

Be Faithful in Prayer

If you are faithful in the practice of prayer, whether it's meditation, immersing yourself in Scripture, or in any other prayer form, it will become easier and easier for you to share your faith with those you teach. The more conscious you are of the presence of God, the more you will want to proclaim it. Remember, God is already attending to you. All you need do is respond.

That's the vision and the message you will want to share with those you teach, and in the following pages we'll explore a number of ways to do this. Some we have already touched upon and some will be new.

For your reflection...

•What is the "vision," the essence of faith for you?

•If you had to put this into one paragraph, could you do it? What would it say?

•Have you ever thought of the Holy Spirit as your personal translator? What feeling does this evoke in you?

•Do you have a regular routine for your personal prayer? Could you begin one?

•What is your favorite prayer word or phrase? How do you use this in your prayer?

•Do you sometimes pray with Scripture? In what ways does this help your teaching?

Let us pray...

Jesus, risen Savior, you are with me always. Help me to be attentive to your presence so that I can more faithfully proclaim it with those I teach. Thank you for the gift of your Holy Spirit who prays for me and within me always. Glory and praise to you, Lord Jesus Christ, now and forever. Amen.

Chapter Two

Praying with Children

We can set up prayer experiences for those we teach, but as we well know, it is God who communicates. We certainly don't have to perfect the art of prayer ourselves before we can pray with children. But in our role as catechists and teachers, we can and should be learning more about prayer even as we pray with those we teach.

We make prayer too complicated! What is prayer anyway? The classic definition is "the lifting of the mind and heart to God." Simplify this by picturing someone you love, one of your children, perhaps, or if you don't have children, a spouse or close friend.

Imagine yourself lifting your mind to that person. What would this mean? Obviously it would mean *paying attention* to the person some of the time.

But at other times it might mean thinking about that person through the day, or just "carrying" that person with you as you go from task to task.

Now imagine yourself lifting your heart to those you love. This might mean doing something loving for them, but it might also mean caring about them and wishing good things for them in a general way throughout the day. It means carrying them around in our hearts.

Carried by God

Now put God in this picture. If prayer is the lifting of the mind and heart to God, it means sometimes paying close attention to God, sometimes consciously loving God, but it also means carrying God around with us in our minds and hearts (or more accurately, being carried around by God), as we go about the ordinary tasks of life.

To pray, or in the words of Saint Paul, "to pray always" simply means walking with God, believing in God's presence, all through the ordinary actions of the day—and sometimes talking to God about them.

Jews at the time of Jesus did not confine their worship to a single location or type of building, or even to a certain time of day. A pious Jew was expected to pray in every place and at every time. "A man [sic] is obliged to recite 100 benedictions each day," the Babylonian Talmud instructed. The believer was expected to bless God throughout the day, and in this way to pray always.

Praying always in part also means "attending to others in whom God dwells." Recall the words of Jesus: "What you do to these little ones of mine, you do to me." When we lift our minds and hearts to those around us, we are in some way lifting our minds and hearts to Jesus and to God.

So you see, prayer is more an attitude than an action. It involves what we are more than what we do. It is our way of being in touch with God and responding to God's love for us.

How to Communicate

There are many ways to do this, and each of us has to discover the way that works best for us. Some catechists and teachers communicate with God best by going to Mass often or prayerfully reading Scripture. Some do it by repeating prayer words they feel comfortable with, like the Jesus prayer, the rosary, or a litany. Others yet do it by writing in a journal addressed to God. Still others pray by placing themselves in the presence of God and consciously opening their minds and hearts to whatever God might communicate. This latter process, as we have already seen, is called meditation, and when people enter it deeply enough, it's also called contemplation.

Again, we should not make this complicated—for ourselves or for those we teach. Meditation involves thinking about God, using Scripture, prayer images, etc., and contemplation is feeling awe at being in the presence of God. Have you ever watched an infant or a beloved child and feel your heart spontaneously contract? That's a moment of contemplation. And we can also experience this in God's presence.

Meditation, with its moments of quiet rest, (which can certainly lead to contemplation), is very important for us as catechists and teachers, but also for those we teach. Thus, I would like to say more about this form of prayer.

Offer Direct Guidance

Look back at the four-step process for meditation on page 7. When you do this process with children, you will usually have to offer them *direct* guidance, invite them to get quiet and still and show them how. You will probably have to lead them in breathing exercises with precise directions. You will also want to find a Scripture story or setting as food for thought. After this preparation, you can then guide children toward an imaginary place where they can meet God, and then you will have to bring them back to where they started. In my experience, after children have done this a few times, they enjoy it and look forward to it. Don't expect immediate cooperation, but do expect quiet.

This exercise, once you have ironed out the wrinkles, takes only ten minutes or so, and teachers who have learned to use it effectively with children find the time well spent. Here is an example of how you might guide children into meditation.

Setting the Stage To begin, offer these instructions, pausing at each "…": Close your eyes and take a deep breath, so deep you can feel your lungs fill up… Now slowly let it out… Breathe deeply three more times. Each time as you breathe in, imagine that God's breath is flowing into you. As you breathe out, let go of your worries, concerns, fears, or problems… Let go of anything but where you are right now—sitting here with God.

Feel yourself relaxing, just be here, focusing on God's Spirit within you.

Imagine now that you are in a special place where it's warm and sunny. See yourself walking along, with no cares or worries, feeling happy and peaceful...

Encountering Jesus Imagine now that you see some-one coming toward you. As the person gets closer, you know in your heart that it is Jesus. He greets you warmly, the way a good friend greets you, and he begins to walk along with you. He asks how you are and how you feel about your life.

Talk to Jesus now about whatever is on your mind. If you are worried about something or some-one, tell him. If you having problems at home or at school, tell him. Say whatever is on your mind...

Now let Jesus speak to you. What might he want to say? Listen to him...

Allow two minutes here.

Now Jesus tells you that he has to move on. Before he goes, however, he invites you to talk to him anytime. He tells you that he loves you very much and treasures your friendship. He says goodbye.

Concluding the Experience Again, breathe deeply three times, breathing in God's Spirit and breathing out your cares and concerns. Now open your eyes back in this setting. (Note: Allow children to talk about this experience if they want to. As a rule, don't ask them to share how they prayed and what they said.)

Obviously, meditation is one very important way to help children listen to God and to hear what God is saying to them personally. But it is only one technique for responding to God in prayer. Others include: 1) group prayer services, 2) litanies of petition and thanksgiving, 3) formal prayers, 4) spontaneous prayer, and 5) prayer rituals. I will say something about each of these now.

Group Prayer Services

There are now many excellent books of such services available today from religious publishers. The services in them usually contain a Scripture passage or story, litany prayers, time for silence, and sometimes a ritual action. If you are using one of these, personalize it and adapt it to your unique group. Involve as many students as possible. Group participation is essential. Don't allow some children to be performers and the others spectators.

Here are several simple guidelines for developing your own group prayer services.

•Invite participation by allowing children to

choose the Scripture, write the petitions, create the banners or posters, compose the litanies, etc.

•Use background music to create an atmosphere of calm and quiet.

•Always allow time for silent prayer.

•Use prayers from the Mass and other liturgical rites. (The liturgy is "under-taught," so use prayers and rituals from it often to reinforce their meaning with children.)

•Keep your services simple and brief, especially at first, limiting them to ten minutes except on special occasions.

Litanies of Petition and Thanks

Litanies are any prayers that follow a pattern and use a repeated response. The General Intercessions at Mass are a typical example. Though asking and saying thanks are the most common form litany prayers take, they can also be used to express sorrow and to offer praise, thus including the four basic prayer groups: praise, petition, thanksgiving, and contrition (or sorrow).

Litanies are the simplest form of class prayer and the easiest to incorporate. However, don't expect children to automatically pray about their needs and concerns. You have to introduce litany prayers just as you do meditation. Ways to do this include:

•Using a class prayer box into which children can anonymously place their prayers.

•Inviting every person in the group to verbalize a petition or say a prayer of thanks or sorrow. Those who don't have specific intentions should be asked to say something generic, like Thank you, Jesus; I praise you, God; or I need you, Holy Spirit.

•Assign two or three children in each class to write prayers for the whole group. These can sometimes be prayers of petition, sometimes prayers of thanks or praise, and sometimes prayers of contrition or sorrow. Use different children each time, so that every child is eventually involved.

•Suggest a response that is repeated after each prayer, for example, We thank you, Jesus; Holy Spirit, please forgive us; or Holy God, we praise your name. Eventually children will lend their voices to your litany prayers, but be patient and don't force the process.

Formal Prayers

There are many beautiful prayers in our Catholic tradition and these also have a place in our class prayer.

Among them are the Our Father, Hail Mary, Glory Be, Act of Contrition, and the prayers of the Mass. If you use formal prayers often, try to keep them from being rote and routine in these ways:

•Divide prayers into parts and have children read them in chorus.

•Chant formal prayers instead of reciting them.

•Invite children to close their eyes and recall the presence of God before you say a formal prayer. Never use formal prayers to silence children.

•Occasionally paraphrase a formal prayer for children so they don't take its meaning for granted. A simple example is the Hail Mary. You might paraphrase it in this way:

Hello Mary, you are fully loved by God and God is always with you. You are the holiest of all women and the baby you carried was holy too. It was Jesus. Dear and good Mary, you are the mother of God, so please pray for us who are still on our journey toward God. Pray for us today and also when we reach the end of our life's journey. Amen.

Spontaneous Prayer

Unlike formal prayers, spontaneous prayers aren't

written down and can't be read off. They come from the heart of the pray-er. Unless a group has built up trust among its members, spontaneous prayer can be a negative experience. Thus a good rule of thumb is to encourage *spontaneous petitions* at first and then eventually invite individual children to sum up the petitions in a closing prayer in their own words. If you *force* children to do this, the prayer is not spontaneous.

Also remember that when you offer time for meditation, children are probably praying spontaneously—only privately. The important thing is that they know that it is very good to talk to God heart to heart, using their own thoughts and words.

For your reflection...

•What are the usual ways that you pray with your class? Do you ever vary this?

•Do you ever lead children in guided meditation? Why or why not? How do they respond?

•Do you allow time in each class for silent prayer? How do the children respond to this?

•Do you ever use prayer services? How do you personalize them? Do you involve children in creating them?

•Have you tried to use litanies with your class? Do you

vary them so that your prayer is more than "asking"?

•What are your favorite formal prayers and how do you pray them in class?

•Is your class comfortable with spontaneous prayer? How can you tell? How can you encourage them to use this type of prayer?

Let us pray...

Loving creator God, I want to pray often and well with those I teach, but I need your Holy Spirit to guide me. Help me to be open to your presence in every moment of my day so that I may be fully present to the children you have entrusted to me. Come Holy Spirit, come with your grace and heavenly aid and rest within me. May I always be a sign of God's patience and care. Amen.

Chapter Three

Prayer and Scripture

In this chapter, we will be talking about helping children listen to God in Scripture. First, however, let's look again at our own attitudes. As catechists whose goal it is to expose children to Scripture and through Scripture to God, what should our personal attitude be?

To answer this, I suggest that each of us must come to terms with two questions: 1) Who is the God of Scripture for us? 2) How will we go about introducing children to this God?

Let's look at the first question: who is the God of Scripture for us? If we consider the whole of Scripture, God seems to have many faces. How do we know which one to share with those we teach?

Is it the "avenging" God who drove Adam and Eve from the garden and who seems to have made the rest of us pay for their sin?

> With sweat on your brow shall you eat your bread... For dust you are and to dust you shall return (Genesis 3:19).

Is it the God of Abraham who destroyed sinners in Sodom and Gomorrah (but who allowed Abraham to bargain)?

> "I am bold indeed to speak like this to my Lord, I who am dust and ashes. But if there are ten good people in Sodom, will you spare it?" God replied, "For the sake of ten, I will not destroy it." But there were not even ten and God destroyed Sodom and Gomorrah with fire and brimstone"
> (Genesis 18:22–33; 19:24).

Is it the God of power and might who led the Israelites out of Egypt and crushed the Pharaoh and his army, and who later gave the people strict commands?

Now at daybreak on the third day there were peals of thunder on the mountain and lightning flashes, a dense cloud, and a loud trumpet blast, and inside the camp all the people trembled (Exodus 19:16).

Is it the God of the prophet Isaiah who seems angry at one moment and appeased the next?

"I God am the keeper of the vineyard. Every moment I water it for fear its leaves should fall; night and day I watch over it. I am angry no longer" (Isaiah 27:3–4).

All of these are faces of our God, but none of them quite fit for us. (I encourage you to look for additional images of God when you have time.) As Christians, we are privileged to have another image of God, one that Jesus himself gave us. It is the God of Jesus that we are called to proclaim. But who is this God?

The God of Jesus

Jesus shows us a *beloved father* (or parent) whom Jesus called ABBA.

"Abba, everything is possible for you. Take this cup away from me, but let it be as you, not I, would have it" (Mark 14:36).

Jesus shows us a *forgiving God* who neither judges nor condemns, but who ceaselessly offers reconciliation. Recall the story of the prodigal son: "The father ran to the boy, clasped him in his arms and kissed him tenderly" (Luke 15:20).

Jesus shows us an *intimate God* who dwells with us through the Holy Spirit.

"Those of you who love me will keep my word and my Father will love you and we shall come to you and make our home with you. The Holy Spirit, whom the Father will send in my name will remind you of all that I have said" (John 14:23,26).

Once we have the image of God that Jesus has given us in our minds and hearts, we can approach all Scripture references knowing that "behind" the text is a God who loves and welcomes us as a loving parent would.

We can then go deeper than the words (which are

influenced by the cultural settings and biases in which they were written) to the God who is speaking through the text to us directly. Even difficult texts like the one about Sodom and Gomorrah will reveal God in a new light when we remember what Jesus has revealed.

If we approach "difficult" texts with the image of God as a loving parent, even texts that are scolding (for example, "Woe to you who are rich"), we will know that the one doing the correcting is doing so for our own good—as loving parents would. When we get angry at our children for doing something wrong, we don't stop loving them, not at all. How much more so with God!

The Second Question

Now let's look at the second question: How can you introduce children to this God who is revealed by Jesus? Traditionally in our catechesis we have used two approaches.

We have offered a broad overview of God's interaction with people, with emphasis on God's mighty deeds, some of which we've already cited. However, when we sweep through Scripture with broad strokes, we tend to emphasize the spectacular, the magical, and the miraculous. These elements are there, but if this is our emphasis, children can logically ask: Why doesn't God do such things today? They conclude that God does not communicate with them. But we know from Jesus that God does communicate with us, and we certainly want those we teach to listen to this God that Jesus has revealed. Thus this first approach is probably not the best choice for catechists.

A second approach is to present isolated Scripture texts about God that support our doctrinal beliefs or support a given lesson. (This is a valid approach and is actually used in many textbooks.) However, knowing *facts about God* through Scripture still doesn't introduce children to a personal God. Scripture quotes may support the points of our lessons, but we shouldn't stop there. We want to reach hearts, not just heads. Our primary goal is to lead children to the God of Jesus, and not merely to doctrinal facts about God.

Let me demonstrate what I mean by giving you a little test. Here are several brief, though significant, Scripture passages. See if you can identify the source—and determine what doctrinal teaching is contained in each.

1. Look, I am coming to save you. When I come, the eyes of the blind will be opened, the ears of the deaf will be unsealed. Then the lame shall leap like a deer and the tongues of the dumb will sing for joy.

Source: _____

Doctrinal Teaching:

_____

_____

2. I am going to speak to your heart and betroth you to myself for ever, and embrace you with integrity and justice, with tenderness and love, and you will come to know that I am your God.

Source: _____

Doctrinal Teaching:

_____

_____

3. I am the resurrection and the life. Those who believe in me, even if they die will live, and whoever lives and believes in me will never die. Do you believe this?

Source: _____

Doctrinal Teaching:

_____

_____

_____

4. Everyone led by the Spirit is a child of God. The Spirit you received does not bring fear, but rather enables you to cry out, Abba Father. The Holy Spirit and your own spirit can then bear united witness that you are a child of God.

Source: _____

Doctrinal Teaching:

_____

_____

How did you do? Let me ask you honestly: what was your attitude when you read these passages? Were you focusing on meeting God through them or on trying to remember the source and the meaning? Did you read them with your head or with your heart? Because I told you this was a test, I predisposed you to read with your head, not your heart, and this is what we tend to do with those we teach when we merely present Scripture as an intellectual back-up for our doctrinal beliefs.

Thus I would like to suggest a third approach for presenting the God of Scripture to those we teach: viewing Scripture as a means for personal communication with God.

Personal Communication

I believe that we should introduce children to the God of Jesus by sharing with them that God is calling them to a personal relationship in which there is regular communication between them and God.

One primary way God communicates with them (and with us) is through the word of Scripture. We should be sharing this with those we teach: every time we read or proclaim Scripture, God is communicating with us. Our goal as catechists is to help those we teach learn to listen to God. Most of us think our goal is to dispense information but there is a big difference between dispensing religious information and preparing and inviting children to relate to God.

In Touch with God

This is a very important point. Our study of Scripture for ourselves and with those we teach is meant to give us a sense of God and put us in closer relationship with God. We won't always understand the passage or the context, for we are not Scripture scholars—but we must be willing to listen. God has already communicated with us; God, according to Jesus, has already taken the first step. God is already in relationship with us. We are invited to listen and respond and to help those we teach to listen and respond.

When we approach Scripture with the attitude that God already loves us, has already forgiven us, and always has open arms to receive us, we are more disposed to hear what God wants to say to us personally. And when we share with children that God already loves them (they don't have to earn God's love), and that God has already forgiven them (they just have to allow themselves to be forgiven), and that God has open arms to receive them, they also will be more disposed to hear what God wants to say to them.

I invite you to look back at the passages on pages 31–32. This time read them slowly and imagine that God is speaking the words to you personally. Read them with an open mind and heart. (Here, by the way, are the correct citations, in the order in which they appear: Isaiah 35:4–6, Hosea 2:19–20, John 11:25–26, Romans 8:14–16.)

You see what a difference this attitude makes? Now the question is: What are some practical ways you can help those you teach begin to listen and respond to the God Jesus has revealed?

A Word of Caution

I am going to suggest three techniques, but before I

describe them, I want to share a word of caution, a word that will keep you from being discouraged if children don't respond to God's communication as you would like them to.

Those you teach are not at the same place on their faith journey as you are. It has taken you "X" number of years to get where you are, and they have not lived through those years and have not had your life experiences. You can't expect them to duplicate *your faith* or *your response* to God in Scripture.

Our role is simply to guide those we teach, to give them experiences of listening to God's Word, so that they will eventually want to do this on their own. We are God's coworkers and witnesses, not enforcers, but we are laying the groundwork, planting the seeds.

So, what are ways we can put children in touch with God's Word in Scripture?

First and foremost, have a special area in your teaching space for prayer where the Bible has an honored place.

In many ancient cultures, every household had a shrine to its gods and goddesses. These were small altars where sacred images were displayed. Some cultures continue this practice today, recognizing the need for sacred space. A special place for prayer in our teaching areas creates a similar environment, one in which children can expect to encounter God in some way. Such special settings can remind us that all space is sacred. When you have a special prayer area in your teaching space, it says to children: Here we do something different, something sacred, something that involves God.

• Begin and end religion class in this place. Process to it and from it, carrying the Bible. Gather around it for prayer and meditation.

• Remind children often that the Bible has an honored place because God speaks to us through its words.

• Make a poster with the words: "God speaks to us in the Bible" or "This is God's Word" and place it in or near your prayer area. Before you read from the Bible, repeat the words on your poster.

Read It with Drama

A second technique for putting children in touch with God through Scripture is to read it reverently and dramatically. If your textbook uses a brief Bible verse (for example, "Sing out your joy to God"), repeat it often during your lesson. Use it as part of your class prayer. Invite children to reflect silently on the words sometime during your class prayer.

•Always recite the Scripture words clearly, distinctly, and dramatically. Don't preach about the meaning of the words, but rather let God speak through them. This is a great temptation for us. We feel duty bound to offer children moral lessons. (For example: "This passage tells us that we should believe that Jesus is the son of God.") Resist this temptation and let children "hear" what God is speaking to them. Assist them more by how you proclaim Scripture than how you explain or analyze it.

If a longer Scripture reading accompanies your lesson, practice it beforehand and try to proclaim it in your own words, rather than stiffly reading it. Or, if you feel more comfortable reading it, do so dramatically. (Keep in mind that drama and gestures add a great deal to a child's recollection of what you proclaim.) Or, even better yet, invite several children to take turns reading sections of the passage.

Re-tell Scripture stories in a contemporary setting, inserting the children into them. For example, in the story about Jesus blessing the children, use your town name and the names of the children in your class. Then give them time to silently reflect about how they felt being a part of this passage.

Have Fun with Scripture

A third technique for putting children in touch with the God of Jesus is to have fun with Scripture. This technique may not directly put children in communication with God, but it does help them get comfortable and familiar with Scripture words and phrases.

After a series of lessons or a unit, play a Jeopardy-type game, giving answers first, based on the Scripture text you have covered. Let the children themselves develop questions and answers based on the Scripture used in your lessons. This might take extra planning, but it's an excellent way to review.

A simpler way to do something similar is to have a Scripture bee with teams. If you have been studying the apostles, you might ask questions like: Who is the tax collector? Who was called a rock? Who was the beloved disciple? (Caution: Whenever you use games, don't put children into competition with one another. Rather, encourage team cooperation to come up with answers.)

Use Scripture quotes or stories in your craft projects and drawing and writing activities.

Have children incorporate Scripture passages into a current news story or an interview.

Invite children to role-play Scripture stories and

do it several times so that every child gets involved. Again, don't preach about the meaning that you think they are supposed to come away with. Just expose them to the words.

Above and beyond all else, pray often with Scripture. If our goal is to discover the God of Jesus and share this discovery with those we teach, we need to open our minds and hearts to this experience. If we never listen to God, we never communicate with God. If we never communicate with God, how can we proclaim the gospel of Jesus Christ?

For your reflection...

•Are you aware of having a particular image of God? What is it and where did you get it?

•How does your image of God compare with the one Jesus revealed?

•In what ways do you use Scripture with those you teach?

•Do your lessons always include quotes or passages from Scripture? How do you emphasize these?

•Is there a special place for the Bible in your class?

•Do you proclaim Scripture reverently and dramatically? Do you encourage children to do the same?

•Do you ever have fun with Scripture? In what ways

and what is the result?

Let us pray...

Come Holy Spirit, open my mind and heart to your Holy Word. Help me to cherish it and proclaim it with deep joy and great enthusiasm. Guide me as I ponder the words of Scripture and try to apply them to my daily decisions and above all to my teaching. Be with me in this and in all things. Amen.

Chapter Four

Prayer and Ritual

In this chapter, I want to offer suggestions for making class prayer more memorable by adding a "ritual" dimension. But before getting down to specifics, let's look at the meaning of the word "ritual." The dictionary says that it is an established form for a ceremony, a system of rites, a ceremonial act or action, any formal and customarily repeated act or series of acts.

The best Catholic example of this is the eucharistic liturgy or Mass. Almost all of the words and actions are prescribed, written down, and an exact order is followed. Because this particular ritual is lengthy, children sometimes have difficulty relating to it. When we use some of the words and prayers from the Mass in our regular classes, however, we are helping children little by little to absorb their meaning.

Still, we shouldn't expect them to value the Mass as an adult would. In its present form, our eucharistic liturgy is certainly a ritual for adults.

Don't Get Upset

Many catechists and teachers get upset when children say that Mass is boring or that they don't like it. But children think that classical music is boring, too, and old movies, and works of art, and historical biographies. We grow into appreciation of such things slowly as we learn more about them, and we often learn to savor them and value them over time.

The Mass is like this. Remember that our role is to guide children toward an experience of God. The Mass is one way they will someday learn to experience God in the midst of a believing community. We can introduce them to it and offer explanations where possible, but we have to leave it to God to speak to their hearts and minds. When children complain that Mass is boring, don't become defensive. Simply say: "I know it seems that way to you now, but as you grow, I hope you will learn that God is among us in a special way at Mass." And just leave it at that.

Other examples of liturgical ritual include the rites for the seven sacraments, which, by the way, are also overlooked as resources for teaching about prayer. If you have access to these rites, you'll find that they offer many possibilities for role-playing or going through the motions of the sacraments. More recently we have been introduced to the rites that are part of the Rite of Christian Initiation for Adults (RCIA). Many of its rituals can be used by catechists who are preparing children for the sacraments, especially eucharist, reconciliation, and confirmation.

But my purpose here is not to elaborate on these official church rituals, but rather to suggest some practical ways you can "ritualize" God's presence in your teaching space. I'm not talking about formalized, written down, prescribed, or primarily liturgical words and movements. Rather, I am thinking of dramatic actions and words that encourage and invite children to participate (particularly in prayer experiences). Let's look more closely at this.

What Is Ritual?

Ritual is *dramatic.* I use this word on purpose. Too many things in life pass by uncelebrated because we don't "mark" or dramatize them. Recall your last religion class. Did you do or say anything dramatic about God, something a child would remember more clearly than anything else? Or, did everything fall into a blurry pattern? I'll offer suggestions shortly.

Ritual uses both *actions and words.* It's important to include dramatic actions because our classes are already too wordy. Think about your own teaching. Who does most of the talking most of the time? And how much class time is devoted to this talking? How much of the talking do children usually recall? What if half your class time was given over to participation? What if there were significant moments of silence? (Silence can be very dramatic!)

This brings me to the final part of my definition. *Encourage and invite participation* (especially to prayer). This follows the axiom that children recall best the things they actually *do.* Ritual gets them *doing* things.

Again, recall your own class. Do children sit most of the time? Do they move around at all (not chaos but controlled movement)? Do you have various "spaces" for various activities? Are there dramatic moments of movement? I realize that many of you teach in restricted spaces, but you can create spaces even within a small room and we'll get to that shortly.

I want to insert the word *repetition* here. While it's not essential to ritual, repetition helps build familiarity. Many children aren't comfortable with certain actions or gestures until they have done them over and over. Repetition is good, very good, but don't overdo it. Get a sense from those you teach whether they want to continue doing something you have introduced or move on to something else.

Now, what are some practical ways that you can celebrate God's presence through ritual with your class? Let me suggest at least four: processions, veneration of the Bible, prayer patterns, and blessings.

Processions and Prayer Spaces

As already emphasized, every religion class should have a prayer space (at least a table or corner). Even in a small room you can set up a tray and cover it with a cloth. The most important item on it should be a Bible, but if you have a bigger table, there are many items you can carry in procession to the prayer space. Processions should always go to and from the prayer space.

If you usually begin your class with prayer, instead of calling to order with a formal prayer, invite children to write or draw something as soon as they arrive that expresses some sentiment toward God: thanks for something that happened, a request for help, sorrow for mistakes, etc. Let them do this while you take roll, make announcements, and wait for late arrivals.

When all have finished, line up by the door or outside the door with each carrying his or her piece of paper or drawing. At this point you should ask for silence. Play a taped piece of music or sing a song (if your group sings). Or simply chant a refrain: "Jesus be with us this day" (repeated over and over until you arrive at the prayer table). Circle the room several times to lengthen your procession.

Have each person place papers or drawings in a designated container and stand or sit around the prayer table. Now conduct your opening prayer. This might be a formal prayer, a prayer service, a time for meditation. It doesn't matter. Always gather in this prayer space.

This kind of dramatic action will help you avoid the temptation to use prayer as a way to quiet children before you teach. (Again, never start prayer to stop noise!) When your prayer is completed, process back to the seating area in silence.

If you normally have a closing prayer, you may want to process to your prayer space as you did for your opening prayer. Also you might want children to carry samples of their work to the prayer area as their prayer offering. There you can bless them and thank God for their efforts.

Eventually you might want to invite children to carry additional items in procession, for example, a Bible, of course, an unlit candle (you can light it once it is firmly on the table), a statue, a poster, flowers, leaves, small stones, artwork, etc. Let children suggest what they want to carry and bring things from home to place on your prayer table.

Veneration of the Bible

I recommend that you always carry the Bible to your prayer space and place it reverently on the table. Children can take turns being the Bible bearers and you can develop a proclamation to be made at the prayer table before the Bible is placed on it, for example, the child holds up the Bible and says, "This is God's Word," and all answer, "Amen."

If possible, always begin your prayer time with a reading from the Bible, perhaps one that is recommended by your textbook lesson or the reading of the day from the *Lectionary for Masses with Children.* If a child is to read it, ask him or her to practice beforehand. If you read it, do so slowly and dramatically. Or ask two or three children to read it in parts.

You might want to sprinkle the Bible with holy water, light a candle next to it, place flowers, leaves, or other items from nature near it, wrap it in a special cloth when it is carried, etc. All of these things say to children: this is a special book, this is God's Word; we treat it in a special way.

Using Prayer Patterns

Litany prayers are an example of a prayer pattern. Here's one way to use these more dramatically. Make up four large posters (avoid buying these by cutting open four large brown grocery bags and ironing them flat). Print one of the four traditional ways to pray on each poster: praise, thanks, sorrow, and asking, and tape the posters to an accessible wall somewhere near your table.

As children offer litany prayers, "Thank you, God"; "Forgive me," etc., have them come forward and stand beside the poster that best describes their prayer. If they have written a litany prayer at the beginning of class have them tape their prayers to the appropriate poster when you arrive at the prayer area.

Another way to do this is to paste the four posters on the four sides of a large appliance box so that it's stationary (easier if the space you use is not also used by others). Children can decorate the box and the posters and write prayers on them, etc. A third way to do this is to have four smaller boxes, like shoe boxes, with one of the prayer words on each. When children come forward to pray, they can pick up the box that best describes their prayer. Make a slit at the top so any written prayers can be slipped inside.

Though very simple, the addition of posters or boxes invites children to move around and to determine what type of prayer they will write or say. This is far more dramatic than standing in place and simply saying a litany prayer, and it encourages children to vary the ways they pray.

Choral Prayers

Other prayer patterns include prayers said in chorus, alternated with prayers said by a leader or several readers. Or prayers said by right-side, left-side groups. As already noted, even formal prayers can be done this way, and it breaks the normal pattern of rote repetition.

Or divide up prayers into phrases and have one child at a time say a phrase. For example, divide the Our Father according to phrases. There will be 10 to 13 of these, depending on how you divide them. Allow every child to say one of the phrases, and practice before this actually becomes your class prayer. When you are ready to pray, invite children to line up in the order they will speak and move to the front of your prayer space as the phrase is said.

Or have children do body motions to the words of a formal prayer. Encourage children themselves to suggest the motions, and again practice them before they are actually used as prayer.

You might be wondering why you should take these extra steps when simple recitation might do. It's still the same prayer, isn't it? Yes, but if your goal is to help the children communicate with God, not just recite words, they need to be as fully involved as possible. You will want them to know that prayer is special and different from other activities, and thus it demands your special effort and attention.

One of my favorite prayer patterns is the giving of blessings, and that's our fourth way to ritualize prayer.

What Are Blessings?

When you give classroom blessings, it simply means that you are "marking something as God's." It's one thing to say that we are God's people, to say that God is present, it's another thing to perform a blessing that acknowledges God's presence. A blessing says: this is sacred, God is here.

Traditionally we Catholics have kept hands off such things. We go to church for blessings and don't even offer them to our spouses and children. And yet, we have been baptized into Christ, we have put on Christ. Why not celebrate this truth daily, hourly? Remember that in the time of Jesus people were encouraged to offer 100 blessings throughout the day.

As catechists you have been commissioned to announce the presence of Jesus and God with your classes. Marking things for God or blessings should be part of this. What types of blessings can you offer?

•*Greeting Blessings* Extend your right hand or both hands toward the children as you pray: "May God be with us today as we gather to learn." "May you hear the voice of Jesus today in this class," etc.

•*Dismissal Blessings* Stand at the door and offer one of these blessings as each child leaves: "May God go with you, children, until we meet again"; "May Jesus walk with you all week long." If you have access to holy water, use it to make a small sign of the cross on each child's forehead or on the palm of the hand. Vary this so it does not become rote.

•*Prayer Time Blessings* An example of this might

be, "May God speak to you now as you listen in silence." Pronounce such blessings slowly and clearly with hands extended in the direction of the children. Devise your own words of blessing and response. Use blessing formulas from the words of the Mass, the sacraments, and the RCIA. For example, "Class is ended, go in peace." All: "Thanks be to God." Or, "May the Lord be with you." All: "And also with you," etc. Occasionally invite the children to offer blessings to one another or to write blessings for parents, family members, parish shut-ins, and to decorate these on special occasions as gifts.

In all these ways you are celebrating God's presence with those you teach. You may object that reading Scripture, praying, and sharing rituals in these ways take valuable class time. Most of the time, if we're honest, however, we would have to say that our words and our textbook lessons are feeding the intellect, but not really touching hearts. Scripture, prayer, and ritual experiences touch hearts and prepare children for a lifelong journey of discovering how to listen to God who is already present in their lives. This is, after all, exactly what we catechists are called to do.

For your reflection..

• Are there certain prayer rituals you always use with your class? How do children respond to them?

• Do you get upset when children don't show interest in religious practices (like going to Mass)?

• Have you ever used the rites or words of the sacraments with your class? Or rituals from the RCIA?

• Are your classes ever dramatic? In what ways?

• Do you encourage full participation in your classes?

• Do you ever carry the Bible in procession? How do children respond to this?

• What prayer patterns do you sometimes use?

• How do children respond when you offer them blessings? Do you ever have them bless one another?

Let us pray...

Gracious and good God, teach me how to pray. Teach me to listen to you and to respond with all my being. Let everything I do and everything I say give witness to your place in my life. Help me to share your presence with those I teach with joy, love, and deep faith. Be with me now and always. Amen.

Year-Round Prayers for Catechists

Here are prayers you can say throughout the year. Each reflects where a typical teacher or catechist might be in any given month. Let these prayers encourage and inspire you to write your own prayers and to pray in season and out, every day and in every situation.

September

Jesus, here I am, beginning again. I ask you to bless the children I will be teaching. Speak through me that I may help them to grow in knowledge, in faith, and in love. Give me patience and understanding, so that through my service to them they may come to know you. Teach me how to pray with them. Amen.

October

Jesus, some of the children in my class are so cooperative and some are so exasperating! I am tempted to favor those who make my task easy. Yet I know that you have given me all of them to teach, and that you love each child as the unique person he or she is. Please share with me your wisdom, your patience, and your love. Amen.

November

Jesus, this is the month for giving thanks. After some of my classes I feel anything but grateful! And yet, there are moments when I see the light of faith and understanding dawning on those I teach. Thank you for my call to be your messenger. Thank you for the children whose gifts as well as shortcomings are helping me to grow. Amen.

December

Jesus, you are the reason for all the excitement this month. Help me to remember this. The children get so carried away by the commercial aspects of Christmas. I want them to know you and to understand that you are God's greatest gift to us. We celebrate Christmas in memory of this. Give me the courage to keep this message before me and before those I teach. Amen.

January

Jesus, this can be such a bleak time of year. All of the holiday festivities are over and winter has settled in. All of the classes I have yet to teach loom before me. Help me to take them one step at a time, to see each one as an opportunity to put children in touch with you. Give me the courage to rededicate myself to helping them grow in faith and understanding. Help me to grow as well. Amen.

February

Jesus, can it be February already? Just when I thought winter would last forever, there have been some bright days on the horizon. The children seem to be getting it together. Some of them actually remember something from class to class. They seem more interested in praying, and they often ask questions that make sense. Help me to love them as you do. Help me to grow in love for you. Amen.

Lenten Prayer

Jesus, you have called me to follow you, from the moment of my baptism until now. As I prepare for the season of Lent, help me to think about my Christian faith and to determine if I am living it the best I can. Please send your Holy Spirit to guide me, and help me to prepare those I teach to walk the lenten journey by your side. Amen.

March

Jesus, I am learning a lot about myself this year. I realize how often I try to control what's going on in the minds and hearts of the children I teach. I want to take personal credit for what they know—or don't know. I'm learning that I have to step back, to let you guide them—at their own pace. This is hard for me, so very hard. Give me patience and understanding. Amen.

April

Jesus, at last another chance to witness some of nature's incredible miracles. The flowers and plants that were "dead" are coming to life again. And this is the month to focus on the new life you experienced when you were raised from death. Easter is a wonderful season. Please help me to convey some of its beauty and wonder to those I teach. Raise them up, Jesus, from the distractions all around them, and help them to believe. Help me to believe, too. Amen.

May

Jesus, this is the month dedicated to your mother, Mary. How fitting this is. May is a lovely and gracious month. I'm feeling happier about my teaching, maybe because it's winding down. But I have learned some important lessons this year, and I hope the children have too. Watch over them this summer as they continue to grow and develop as people of faith. Give them the gift of courage and help them to remember that you are with them always. Help me to remember, too. Amen.

Of Related Interest...

Prayer Services for Catechist & Teacher Meetings
Gwen Costello
These 30 services give a complete prayer experience that teaches
valuable faith lessons. 0-89622-696-4, 72 pp, $12.95 (M-77)

Praying with the Saints
30 Classroom Prayer Service for Children
Gwen Costello
These prayer services and activities focus on an aspect of a saint's life
that children (grades 3-6) can imitate. 0-89622-982-3, 104 pp, $12.95 (J-30)

Reconciliation Services for Children
18 Prayer Services to Celebrate God's Forgiveness
Gwen Costello
Ready-to-use services that help prepare children in grades 2-6 to receive
the sacrament of reconciliation. 0-89622-516-X, 72 pp, $12.95 (B-83)

Junior High Prayer Services by Themes and Seasons
Gwen Costello
These 21 prayer services addess contemporary dilemmas and church
seasons and offer students (grades 6-8) opportunities to reflect, pray,
and respond to one another and to God. 1-58595-106-4, 88 pp, $12.95 (J-67)

Classroom Prayer Services for the Days of Advent and Lent
Gwen Costello
These sixty creative services for children (ages 7-10) celebrate God's presence through veneration of the Bible, prayer patterns, speaking parts,
guided meditations, and blessings. 0-89622-737-5, 144 pp, $12.95 (B-39)

A Prayerbook for Catechists
Gwen Costello
Offers prayers from the heart for a variety of seasons and situations.
0-89622-979-3, 48 pp, $5.95 (J-26)

TWENTY-THIRD PUBLICATIONS
185 WILLOW STREET • PO BOX 180 • MYSTIC, CT 06355
TEL: 1-800-321-0411 • FAX: 1-800-572-0788
Bayard E-MAIL: ttpubs@aol.com • www.twentythirdpublications.com